JOHN JACOBSON'S

Patriotic Partners

A Collection of Partner Songs for Young Singers

Arranged by Tom Anderson

TABLE OF CONTENTS

	Piano/	…eet
America for Me (with *America, the Beautiful*)	4	36
Give Love (with *Down by the Riverside*)	6	38
Have You Ever Seen a Yankee Doodle? (with *Yankee Doodle Boy*)	10	41
I Love America (with *Home Sweet Home*)	13	43
I Love That Grand Old Flag (with *You're a Grand Old Flag*)	18	46
Let Freedom Ring (with *America*)	22	48
There's a Light (with *Simple Gifts*)	27	51
Three Cheers for America! (with *Hip Hip Hooray for the U.S.A.*)	30	53

An **ENHANCED CD** is also available separately or in a kit with the Teacher Edition. The CD includes audio song files and data files for the Amazing Slow Downer and PDF files of the singer songsheets so you can project them. The CD can be played in a regular CD player or through your computer. Each computer is set up a little differently. Your computer may automatically open the audio CD portion of this enhanced CD and begin to play it. To access the data files from a **PC**, click on My Computer, then right click on the Drive that you placed the CD in. Click Open. You should then see a folder named "PDF files" and a folder named "Amazing Slow Downer." **MAC** users will see 2 icons: "audio CD" and "PDf files and ASD." Download free Adobe Reader from www.adobe.com to open the data files.

Visit Hal Leonard Online at
www.halleonard.com

Objectives and National Standards for "Patriotic Partners"

The complete National Arts Standards and additional materials relating to the Standards are available from MENC: **www.menc.org**.

America for Me (found on pages 4-5)

OBJECTIVES

- Sing in tune
- Sing a partner song and maintain pitch and steady beat
- Compare and contrast melody lines
- Develop an appreciation of the United States and its heritage
- Describe appropriate audience behavior during patriotic songs (remove hats, etc.)

*This lesson addresses the National Standards for Arts Education, Music Grades **K–4**: 1d, 1e, 6c, 6e, 9c, 9e.*

*This lesson addresses the National Standards for Arts Education, Music Grades **5–8**: 1a, 1c, 1d, 6b, 9c.*

Give Love (found on pages 6-9)

OBJECTIVES

- Sing in tune
- Sing a partner song and maintain pitch and steady beat
- Identify and sing a syncopated rhythm
- Identify distinguishing characteristics of spirituals

*This lesson addresses the National Standards for Arts Education, Music Grades **K–4**: 1a, 1c, 1d, 5a, 6b, 6e, 9a, 9b.*

*This lesson addresses the National Standards for Arts Education, Music Grades **5–8**: 1a, 1c, 1d, 5a, 6b, 8b, 9a, 9c.*

Have You Ever Seen a Yankee Doodle? (found on pages 10-12)

OBJECTIVES

- Sing in tune
- Sing a partner song and maintain pitch and steady beat
- Compare and contrast melody lines
- Visually and aurally recognize a repeated melodic line

*This lesson addresses the National Standards for Arts Education, Music Grades **K–4**: 1a, 1b, 1d, 1e, 5b, 6b, 6c, 6e.*

*This lesson addresses the National Standards for Arts Education, Music Grades **5–8**: 1a, 1c, 1d, 5a, 6a, 6c.*

I Love America (found on pages 13-17)

OBJECTIVES

- Sing in tune
- Sing a partner song and maintain pitch and steady beat
- Sing expressively with correct phrasing and diction
- Sing and read dotted quarter–eighth rhythms
- Develop an appreciation of the United States and its heritage

*This lesson addresses the National Standards for Arts Education, Music Grades **K–4**: 1a, 1b, 1c, 1d, 1e, 5d.*

*This lesson addresses the National Standards for Arts Education, Music Grades **5–8**: 1a, 1d, 5a, 6c.*

I Love That Grand Old Flag (found on pages 18-21)

OBJECTIVES

- Sing in tune
- Sing a partner song and maintain pitch and steady beat
- Sing and identify rests on a downbeat
- Compare and contrast repeated melodic/rhythmic lines
- Develop an appreciation of the United States and its heritage

*This lesson addresses the National Standards for Arts Education, Music Grades **K–4**: 1a, 1d, 1e, 5a, 6c, 6e, 9c, 9e.*

*This lesson addresses the National Standards for Arts Education, Music Grades **5–8**: 1a, 1c, 1d, 5a, 6a, 6b, 6c, 9c.*

Let Freedom Ring (found on pages 22-26)

OBJECTIVES

- Sing in tune
- Sing a partner song and maintain pitch and steady beat
- Play a countermelody on chimes and maintain a steady beat
- Demonstrate the beat pattern of strong and weak beats in $^{3}/_{4}$ meter
- Discuss the terms Introduction and Coda

*This lesson addresses the National Standards for Arts Education, Music Grades **K–4**: 1a, 1d, 1e, 2a, 2b, 2f, 5a, 6b, 6c, 6e.*

*This lesson addresses the National Standards for Arts Education, Music Grades **5–8**: 1a, 1d, 2a, 2c, 5a, 6a, 6c.*

There's a Light (found on pages 27-29)

OBJECTIVES

- Sing in tune
- Sing a partner song and maintain pitch and steady beat
- Identify melodic direction
- Compare and contrast melody and harmony lines
- Discuss Shaker life and communities and the importance of music in the community

*This lesson addresses the National Standards for Arts Education, Music Grades **K–4**: 1c, 1d, 1e, 5d, 6b, 6c, 6e, 9b, 9d.*

*This lesson addresses the National Standards for Arts Education, Music Grades **5–8**: 1a, 1c, 1d, 6a, 6b, 9c.*

Three Cheers for America! (found on pages 30-34)

OBJECTIVES

- Sing in tune
- Sing a 3-part song and maintain pitch and steady beat
- Compare and contrast melody lines
- Read a syncopated rhythm
- Develop the ability to evaluate the quality of their performance in rehearsal

*This lesson addresses the National Standards for Arts Education, Music Grades **K–4**: 1a, 1d, 1e, 2a, 2b, 2f, 5a, 6b, 6e, 7a.*

*This lesson addresses the National Standards for Arts Education, Music Grades **5–8**: 1a, 1d, 2a, 2c, 5a, 6a, 6c, 7b.*

1/9

America for Me

(with *America, the Beautiful*)

By JOHN JACOBSON
Arranged by TOM ANDERSON

Scoop R hand low to high
Clasp hands together overhead
Burst hands high to low with palms up
Present Jazz hands low
mer - i - ca! God shed His grace on thee. And crown thy good with
1 Clap burst on downbeat
Reach L Blade hand up, then R
Clap overhead
Bring clasped hands to chest
R hand to heart
bright as the sun. I see a peo - ple liv - ing as one. Look in my heart and
Cm7 F7 Cm7 F7 Cm7 F7 A♭(add9)/B♭ B♭13 E♭ Cm7
12
Grab hands with neighbors on both sides
Raise held hands to overhead
Lower hands
broth - er-hood, from sea to shin - ing sea.
Point R hand at audience
Salute
you ought to see A - mer - i - ca for
B♭/D B♭ Cm7 Cm7/F F7 B♭ F7 Cm7 Cm7/F F7
16
Raise held hands to overhead
O sea to shin - ing sea.
Finish salute
Grab hands with neighbors and raise them to overhead, like Part I
me! mer - i - ca for me!
B♭ F7 Cm7/F F7 B♭ Cm/F B♭ B♭/F F/A B♭ N.C.
20
8vb
loco

Give Love

(with *Down by the Riverside*)

By JOHN JACOBSON
Arranged by TOM ANDERSON

Lively (♩ = 160) (♫ = ♩♪ triplet)

Am7 Am9/D D9 G C/G G

Piano

5 2 times

Partner 1

2 claps at chest level *Reach both hands to audience* *L hand to heart* *R hand to heart*

Sing both times

Hey, (clap, clap) a lit - tle love-'ll do ya! That's what it's all a-

Partner 2

Sway L *Snap* *Sway R* *Snap* *Sway L* *Snap* *Back to center* *Clap on rest* *Point R hand downstage R*

Sing 2nd time only

lay down my sword and shield down by the

G

5

cont. sim.

Plié *2 claps at chest level* *Reach both hands to audience*

bout! Hey (clap, clap) a lit - tle love-'ll do ya!

Clap *Point R hand downstage R* *Clap*

riv - er - side, down by the riv - er - side,

D7

8

Fold (clasp) hands
Twist wrists to open hands up to a shrug
13
Claps at chest level
Turn hate in - side out!
Hey, (clap, clap) a
Point R hand downstage R
Sway snap
L R
down by the riv - er - side. Gon-na lay down my
G
11
Reach both hands to audience
Shrug
Plié
lit - tle love-'ll do ya! What's all the fight - ing for?
L
Clap
Point R hand downstage R
sword and shield down by the riv - er - side and
14
Both hands to heart
Plié
Mini whack attach
Clap
Slap R leg
Slap L leg
Clap
Oh yeah, a lit - tle love - 'll give you more than a lit - tle bit
Both hands to heart
Relevé
Wipe a la "safe"
stud - y war no more.
D7
G
17

Thumbs up
21
Clap
Reach R hand to audience
Clap twice X
X
Reach L hand to audience
Clap twice X
more. Give love! Give love!
Clap on the beats Part I is not clapping on
X X X X
I ain't gon - na stud - y war no more. I ain't gon - na
G7
C
20
X
Slap hands to thighs
Hold heart in both hands and rock
L R
Give love one more chance. Oh, won't you give love
Same as part I and rock
X X X X L R
stud - y war no more, stud - y
G
D7
23
L R
Mini whack attach
Clap Slap R Slap L Clap
Snap fingers of both hands on beat 1
one more, one more it - ty bit - ty chance. Oh, won't you
L R
Slap thighs
Mini whack attach
Clap Slap R Slap L Clap
war no more. I ain't gon - na
C(add9)/D D7 G G7
26

29
Clap
Reach R hand to audience
Clap twice
X X
Reach L hand to audience
Clap twice
X X
Slap hands to thighs
Give love! Give love! Give love one more chance.
As before, clap when Part 1 doesn't
X X X X X X
stud - y war no more. I ain't gon - na stud - y war no more,
C
G
29
Hold heart in both hands and rock side to side
L R L R
Oh, won't you give love one more,
Hold heart in both hands and rock side to side
X X
L R L R
stud - y war no
Em
Am7
Am9/D
D9
32
Mini whack attach
Clap Slap R Slap L Clap
Snap fingers on beat 1
Mini whack attach
Clap Slap R Slap L Clap
Snap fingers on beat 1
Fold arms over chest and nod
1
2
one more it - ty bit - ty chance! one more it - ty bit - ty chance!
DOWN BY THE RIVERSIDE
African-American Spiritual
Same as Part 1
Mini whack attack
Fold arms over chest and nod
Gon - na more.
G
G
N.C.
35

Have You Ever Seen a Yankee Doodle?

(with *Yankee Doodle Boy*)

By JOHN JACOBSON
Arranged by TOM ANDERSON

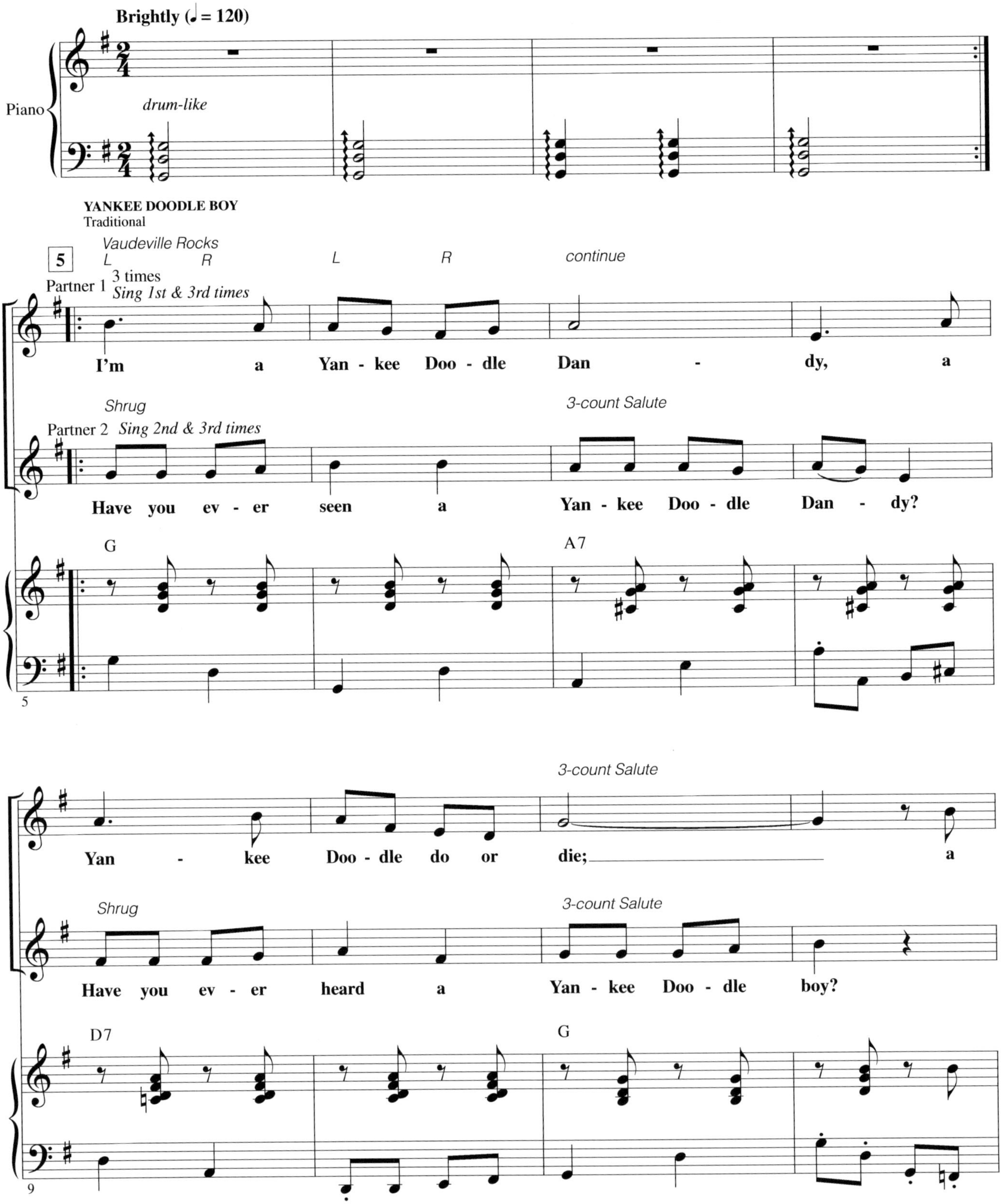

Brightly (♩ = 120)

Piano

drum-like

YANKEE DOODLE BOY
Traditional

5

Vaudeville Rocks
L R L R *continue*

Partner 1 3 times *Sing 1st & 3rd times*

I'm a Yan - kee Doo - dle Dan - dy, a

Shrug *3-count Salute*

Partner 2 *Sing 2nd & 3rd times*

Have you ev - er seen a Yan - kee Doo - dle Dan - dy?

G A7

3-count Salute

Yan - kee Doo - dle do or die; a

Shrug *3-count Salute*

Have you ev - er heard a Yan - kee Doo - dle boy?

D7 G

13
Stop Marches
L L L L
real, live nephew of my Uncle Sam's,
Opera hands and lean L
Lean R
He can sing a song as sweet as cotton candy.
E7 Am E7 Am
Regular March
L R L R
3-count Salute
born on the Fourth of July! I've
Same as Part 1
He was born his Uncle's pride and joy.
A9 D7
17
21
Hold heart and lean L
Hold heart and lean R
got a Yankee Doodle sweetheart,
Shrug
3-count Salute
If you ever see a Yankee Doodle Dandy,
G A7

Hold heart and lean L
Hold heart and lean R
29
Spirit of '76 March
she's my Yan - kee Doo - dle joy.
Yan - kee Doo - dle
Shrug
3-count Salute
Point R hand to audience
if you ev - er hear a Yan - kee Doo - dle boy, you will
D7
G
G5
Pretend to ride a pony
Thumbs to self
came to Lon - don just to ride the po - nies, I am that Yan - kee Doo - dle
Pretend to ride a pony
Thumbs to self
know it's me up - on that po - ny; I am that Yan - kee Doo - dle
A7
D7
3-count Salute
3-count Salute
boy.
boy.
3-count Salute
3-count Salute
boy. Oh, boy!
boy. Oh, boy!
N.C.
8va
G
G
G

4/12 I Love America
(with *Home, Sweet Home*)

By JOHN JACOBSON
Arranged by TOM ANDERSON

rit.
end Solo
I will count my bless - ings as I proud - ly say:
Eb2/G
Ab6/9
Fm7
Bb7sus
Bb7
rit.
14
18
Melody Instrument
Play 2nd time only
a tempo
In 3-group peel-off, place R hand over heart on your number
①
②
Partner 1 Sing both times
a tempo
"I love A - mer - i - ca. I love A-
Scoop both hands low to high
Pull fists slowly to shoulder height
Partner 2 Sing 2nd time only
Give me your tired your poor, your hud - dled mass - es yearn - ing to breath
18
Eb(add9)
Fm/Eb
Eb
Ab6/9/Eb
Eb/Ab
a tempo
18
③
mer - i - ca. I love A - mer - i - ca, my
Burst both hands out and down
Slowly wipe hands out like "safe"
free. The wretch - ed re - fuse of your teem - ing shore, send
Eb/Bb
Bb7
Eb2/G
Eb/Ab
21

26
Present R hand L to R
Repeat peel-off, hands to heart
1
home, sweet home. I love A-
Bring both hands to heart
Scoop R fist low to high
these, the home-less temp-est tossed to me. I lift my lamp be-side your
26
Fm7
A♭(add9)/B♭
B♭13
E♭2
24
2
3
mer - i-ca. I love A - mer - i-ca. I love A-
Open R fist and let it float down
gold - en door. I lift my lamp be-side your gold - en
E♭/A♭
A♭6
Fm7
E♭2/G
Bdim7
Cm7
Cm9/B♭
27

Play
Present R hand L to R
mer - i - ca, our home, sweet home."
Scoop both hands from low to audience
door; wel - come home, sweet
A♭6 E♭/G Fm7 Fm7/B♭ B♭13 E♭(add9) A♭(add9)
add melody instrument
31
3-group peel-off, hand to heart
home." I love A - mer - i - ca.
Bring hands to heart
home. Home, sweet
Fm7 Fm9/B♭ E♭(add9) A♭(add9) B♭sus
35

②
I love A - mer - i - ca.
③
I love A - mer - i - ca.
Burst both hands out and down
home.
Home, sweet
Scoop L
home.
Home, sweet
E♭
E♭/A♭
A♭6/B♭
E♭(add9)
A♭(add9)
B♭sus
39
Bring L hand up to join R hand over heart
I love A - mer - i - ca.
On final chord, all look up over audience's head
Scoop R
home.
Home, sweet
Bring both hands to cover heart
home.
E♭
E♭/A♭
A♭6/B♭
E♭(add9)
let ring
43
Ped.

I Love That Grand Old Flag

(with *You're a Grand Old Flag*)

By JOHN JACOBSON
Arranged by TOM ANDERSON

13
Half time march
L
R
L
R
em - blem of the land I love, the
Salute
Hands on knees and bounce, watch parade L to R
thir - teen stripes of red and white; you'll nev - er see a fin - er sight,
Am7
D7
G
B7
Em
13
Regular march
L
R
L
R
3-count Salute
home of the free and the brave.
Ev - 'ry
Wag R index finger at audience
Salute
Wipe brow with R hand
(spoken)
ev - en if you live to be a hun - dred for - ty two! Whew!
A7
D7
17
21
Stop Marches
L
L
L
L
heart beats true 'neath the red, white and blue, where there's
R hand to heart
Wag R finger moving it from L to R
Proud to be an A - mer - i - can; fa - ther, moth - er, daugh - ter, son!
G
C
G
D7
G
21

Regular march
L R L R
3-count Salute
nev - er a boast or brag. But should
Wave R hand like "come on"
3-count Salute
Come a - long, there's al - ways room for ev - 'ry - one.
E7
Am
D7
25
29
Step forward with L foot and clasp praying hands. This could be in a 3-group peel-off.
Stand straight, hands to sides
auld ac - quain - tance be for - got, keep your
L Blade hand high
R Blade hand high
L hand down
R hand down
The red, the white, the blue; all right!
G D G Am7 D7
29
Salute
Finish 3-count salute
1
eye on the grand old flag.
A7 C/D D7 G N.C. D7
33

2
You're a
Salute
Finish 3-count salute
I just love that grand old flag!
A7
C/D
D7
G
D7
37
Salute
3
(Everyone)
Reach into back pocket and
pull out a small American flag
Wave
flag
eye on the grand old flag!
Salute
I just love that grand old flag!
A7
C/D
D7
G
N.C.
41

6/14 Let Freedom Ring

(with *America*)

By JOHN JACOBSON
Arranged by TOM ANDERSON

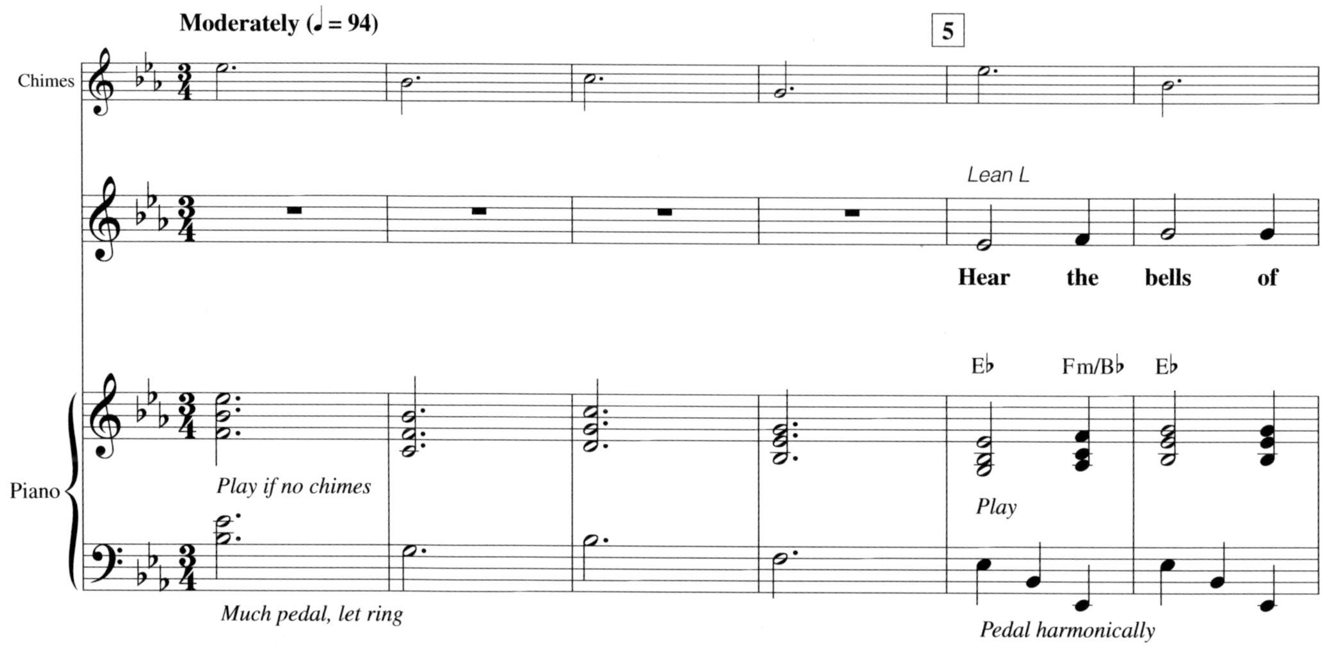

13
Hold hands with neighbors
sing. Now hand in hand, a - cross this great land, we
B♭7sus B♭7 Fm7 Fm7/B♭ B♭/A♭ E♭/G Fm7sus E♭ Cm7sus
12
rit.
Lift held hands
lift our voice and proud - ly sing!
Let ring
Fm7 E♭/G A♭(add9) B♭7sus B♭7
17
AMERICA – Traditional Music
Words by SAMUEL FRANCIS SMITH
22
3 times
Play 3rd time only
a tempo
R hand over heart
3 times
Partner 1 Sing 1st & 3rd times
My coun - try 'tis of thee, sweet land of
Clasp Prayer hands at chest level and slowly raise them
Partner 2 Sing 2nd & 3rd times
Let there be peace in our
E♭ Cm Fm/A♭ B♭7 Cm7 B♭/D E♭ Cm A♭
22

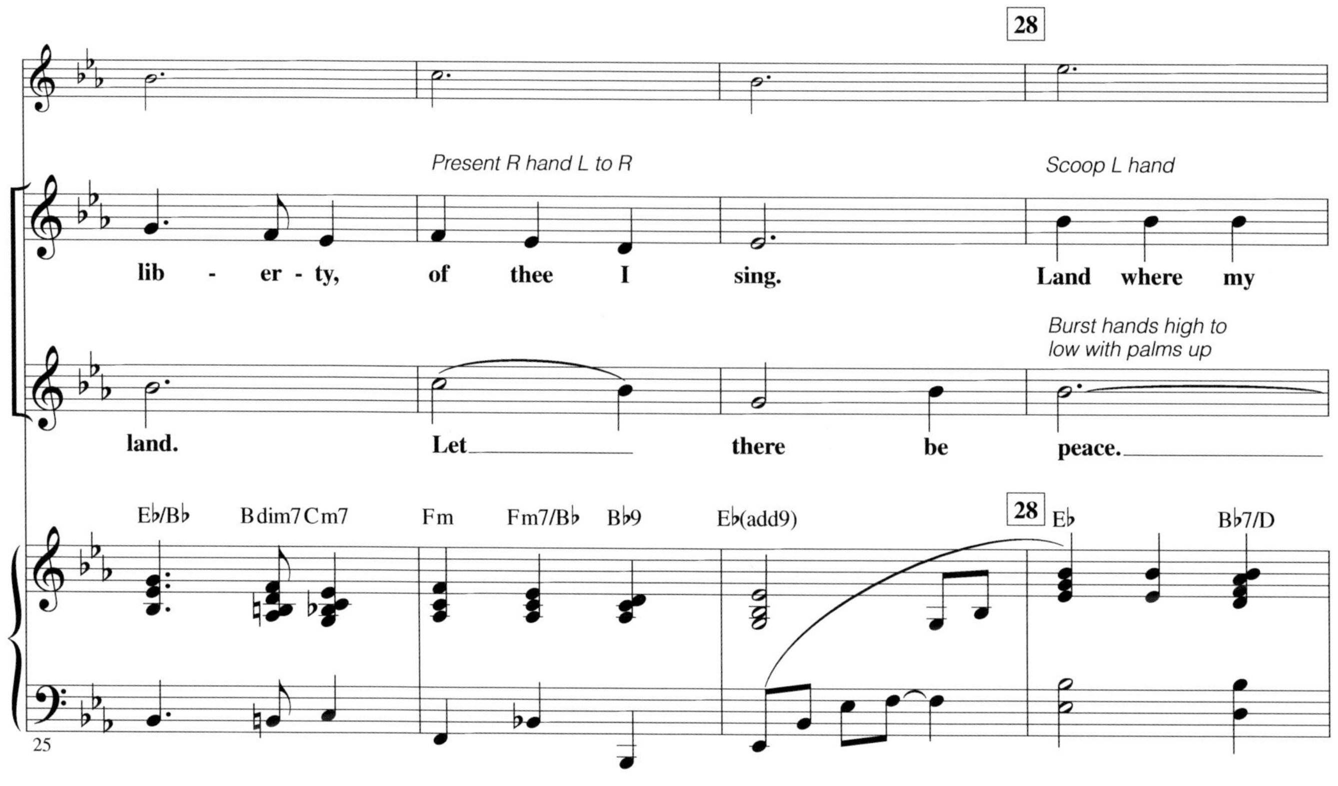
28
Present R hand L to R
Scoop L hand
lib - er - ty, of thee I sing. Land where my
Burst hands high to low with palms up
land. Let there be peace.
E♭/B♭ Bdim7 Cm7 Fm Fm7/B♭ B♭9 E♭(add9)
28
E♭ B♭7/D
25

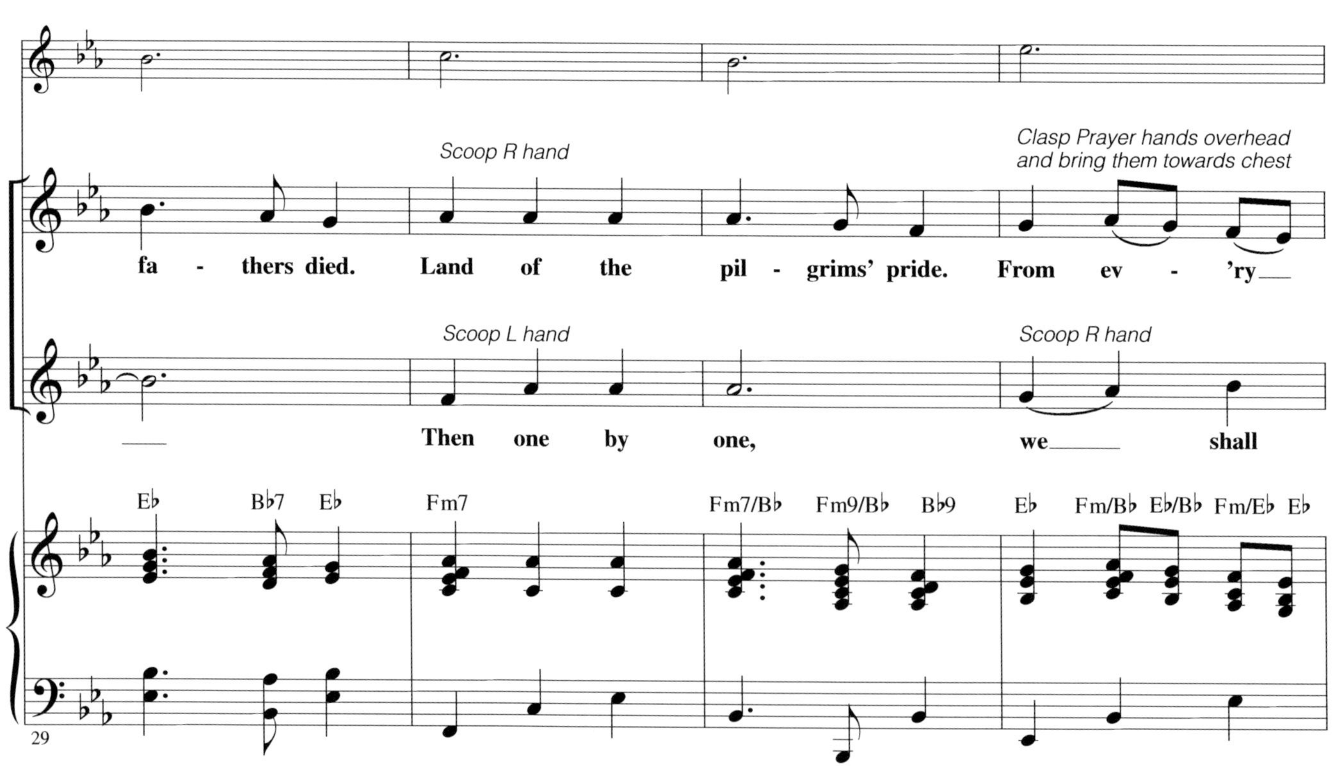
Scoop R hand
Clasp Prayer hands overhead and bring them towards chest
fa - thers died. Land of the pil - grims' pride. From ev - 'ry
Scoop L hand
Scoop R hand
Then one by one, we shall
E♭ B♭7 E♭ Fm7 Fm7/B♭ Fm9/B♭ B♭9 E♭ Fm/B♭ E♭/B♭ Fm/E♭ E♭
29

1
Burst hands high to low with palms up
1
moun - tain-side, let___ free - dom ring.
Clasp Prayer hands overhead
and bring them towards chest
see that we can be
Fm7 E♭/G A♭ E♭/B♭ B♭9 E♭6/9 Fm7sus/B♭
Let ring
Let ring
33
2
2
Burst hands high to low with palms up
free.
E♭6/9 Fm7sus/B♭ E♭6/9 Fm7sus/B♭
cont. sim.
Let ring
cont. sim.
37

45
Burst hands high to low with palms up
Hold hands in long lines
ring. Let free-
Burst hands high to low with palms up
Hold hands in long lines
free. We can
45
E♭6/9 Fm7sus/B♭ E♭6/9 Fm7sus/B♭ E♭/B♭
Let ring
cont. sim.
41
Let ring
dom ring.
be free.
B♭9 8va E♭ Fm/B♭ B♭/E♭ Fm7/B♭ E♭6/9
loco
46
8vb Let ring

7/15

There's a Light

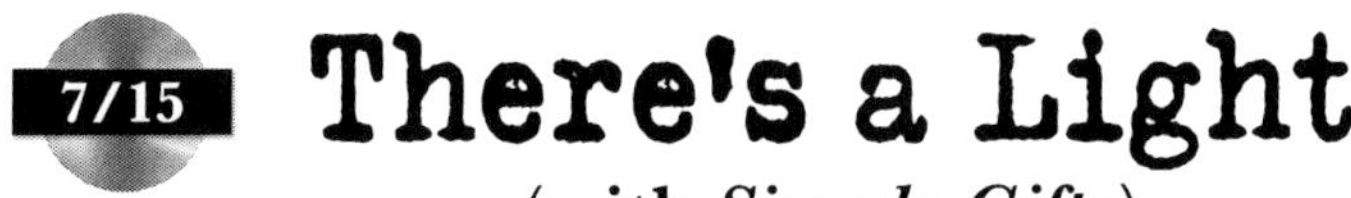

(with *Simple Gifts*)

By JOHN JACOBSON
Arranged by TOM ANDERSON

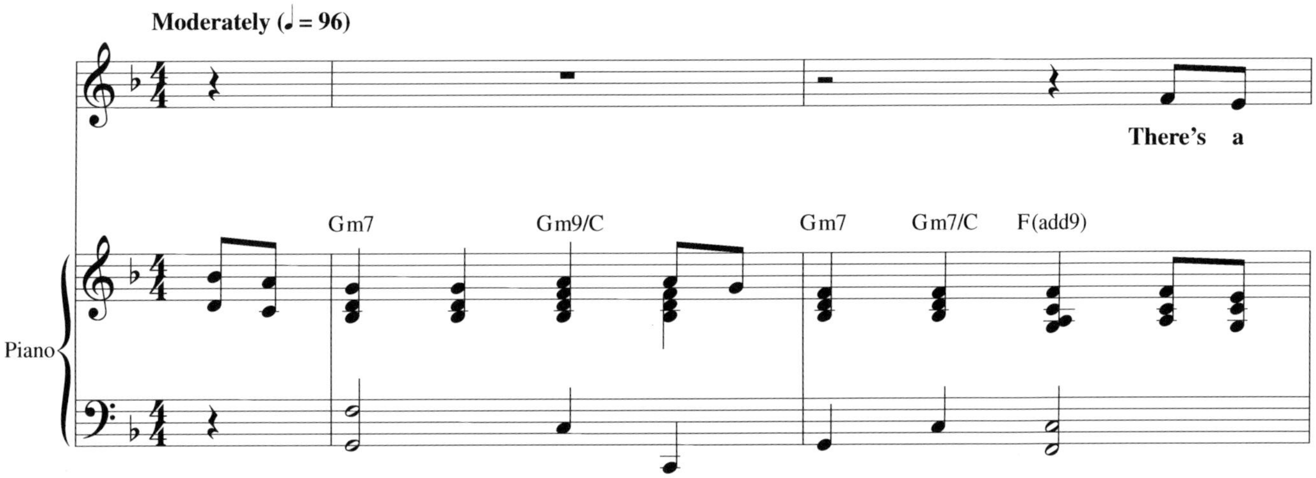

Moderately (♩ = 96)
There's a
Gm7
Gm9/C
Gm7
Gm7/C
F(add9)
Piano

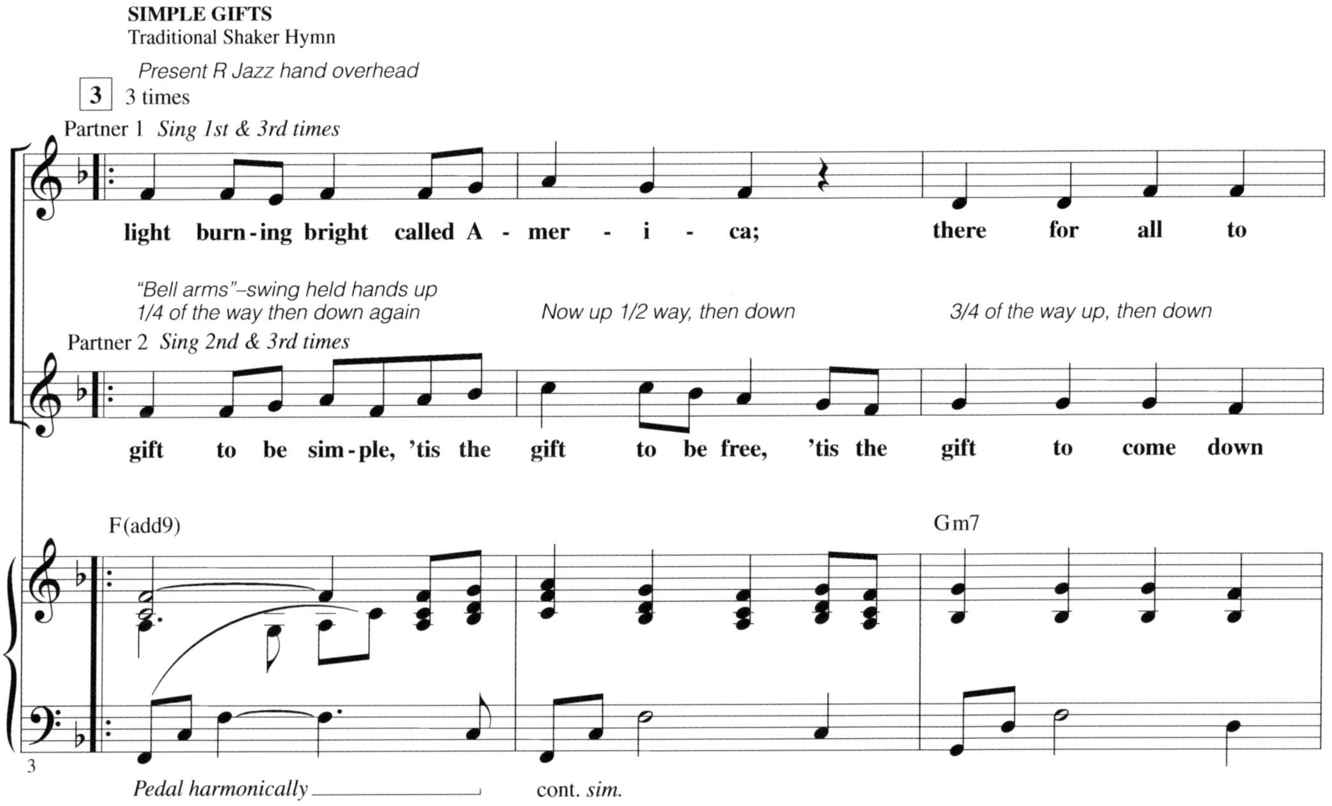

SIMPLE GIFTS
Traditional Shaker Hymn
Present R Jazz hand overhead
3
3 times
Partner 1 Sing 1st & 3rd times
light burn-ing bright called A - mer - i - ca; there for all to
"Bell arms"–swing held hands up 1/4 of the way then down again
Now up 1/2 way, then down
3/4 of the way up, then down
Partner 2 Sing 2nd & 3rd times
gift to be sim-ple, 'tis the gift to be free, 'tis the gift to come down
F(add9)
Gm7
3
Pedal harmonically
cont. sim.

Shimmy R hand
see. It can shine like a sign show-ing ev - 'ry one that
Swing held hands all the way up and keep them up
Wave held hand gently overhead
L R L R
where we ought to be, and when we find our-selves in the place just right, 'twill
Gm7/C C5 F(add9)
6
Burst R hand high to low
11
Tilt heads in opposite direction of Part 2
R L
we can all live free. Let us give thanks for
Lower hands slowly
Keep holding hands, tilt heads
L R
be in the val - ley of love and de-light. When true sim-
Gm7 Gm7/C Gm7 Gm7/C C9 F(add9)
9
R L R L R L
sim - ple gifts. Let us give thanks for the land we love.
L R L R L R
pli - ci - ty is gained, to bow and to bend we shan't be a-shamed. To
Gm7 C7sus C5
12

Point R hand low to high
Shimmy R Jazz hand overhead
Look in your heart and let your A - mer - i - can light keep shin - ing,
Lift held hands slowly to overhead
Lower hands slowly
turn, turn will be our de-light, till by turn - ing, turn - ing we
F(add9)
Gm7
Gm9/C
15
Burst R hand high to low
1
2
shin - ing bright.
There's a
Hold hands in long lines
'Tis the come 'round right. 'Tis the
Gm7
Gm7/C
F(add9)
18
Burst R hand high to low
All do a small bow
3
rit. to end
shin - ing bright.
Let go of held hands
come 'round right.
Gm7
Gm7/C
F(add9)
rit. to end
20

Three Cheers for America!

(with *Hip Hip Hooray for the U.S.A.*)

By JOHN JACOBSON
Arranged by TOM ANDERSON

4-measure drum roll-off on recording

With pride (♩ = 120)

Clap twice — *All shout*

Hip hip hoo - ray!

Punch R fist into the air

N. C.

Clap twice

Hip hip hoo - ray!

Punch R fist into the air

Hoo- ray for the U. S. A.!

Salute — *3-count Salute*

There's

Piano

9 𝄋

Tilting claps L R L R — 4 times — *3-count Salute*

Partner 1 *Sing 1st & 4th times (D.S.)*

no place I like bet - ter than A mer - i - ca! There's

Swing R "rah rah" fist across front 4 times ① ② ③ ④

Partner 2 *Sing 2nd & 4th times (D.S.)*

"Three cheers for A - mer - i - ca!

Punch R fist into the air 4 times ① ② ③ ④

Partner 3 *Sing 3rd & 4th times (D.S.)*

Hip hip hoo - ray for the U. S. A.! Oh,

9 𝄋 B♭

Tilting claps
L R L R
3-count Salute
no place I would rath - er stay. So
Salute
3-count Salute
Stand up proud and tall!
Slap thighs
Clap on beat 2
Slap thighs
Clap
3-count Salute
hip hip hoo - ray to - day! We're proud to
F7 E♭/F F E♭/F
13
17
Swing R "rah rah" fist across front 4 times
① ② ③ ④
let's give a cheer to the land we love. Let the
Punch R fist overhead 4 times
① ② ③ ④
Three cheers for A - mer - i - ca;
Tilting claps
L R L R
Slap thighs
Clap
Punch R fist up
be in a land where we all live free, so
17
B♭
17

Tilting claps
L R L R
(4th time) To Coda
Slap thighs
Clap
Punch R fist into the air
whole world hear us say:
Slap thighs
Clap
Slap thighs
Clap
Slap thighs
Clap
Punch R fist into the air
sing out one and all!"
Swing R "rah rah" fist twice
hip hip hoo - rah and hoo -
(4th time) To Coda
Cm7
F7
1 B♭
2 B♭
21
Slap thighs
Clap
Punch R fist up
(All parts) Clap twice
Punch fist up
All shout
29
All to - geth - er now! Hip hip hoo - ray!
Slap thighs
Clap
Punch R fist up
All shout
All to - geth - er now! Hip hip hoo - ray!
Slap thighs
Clap
Punch R fist up
All shout
ray! All to - geth - er now! Hip hip hoo - ray!
3 B♭
29
N. C.
27

Clap twice
Punch fist up
Salute
3-count Salute
D.S. al Coda
Hip hip hoo - ray! Hoo - ray for the U. S. A.!
There's
Hip hip hoo - ray! Hoo - ray for the U. S. A.!
Hip hip hoo - ray! Hoo - ray for the U. S. A.!
D.S. al Coda
31
Slap thighs
Clap
Punch R fist up
Tilting claps
CODA
39
L
R
L
R
say, let the whole world hear us
Slap thighs
Clap
Punch R fist up
Slap thighs
Clap
Slap thighs
Clap
all! Sing out one and
Slap thighs
Clap
Punch R fist up
"Rah Rah" fist twice
1
2
ray! Hip hip hoo - rah and hoo-
CODA
39
B♭
Cm7
F7
37

Slap thighs
Clap
Punch R fist up
Tilting claps
L R L R L R
say, let the whole world hear
Slap thighs
Clap
Punch R fist up
Slap thighs Clap
Slap thighs Clap
Punch R fist up
all! Sing out one
Slap thighs
Clap
Punch R fist up
"Rah Rah" fist twice
Slap thighs Clap
ray! Hip hip hoo - rah and
B♭
Cm7
Cm7sus/F
41
L R
Wave R hand overhead
Clap twice
All shout
Punch R fist up
us say: Hip hip hoo - ray!
Wave R hand overhead
Clap twice
All shout
Punch R fist up
and all! Hip hip hoo - ray!
Punch R fist up
Wave R hand overhead
Clap twice
All shout
Punch R fist up
hoo - ray! Hip hip hoo - ray!
F7
B♭
N. C.
46

Student Songsheets

PDFs of Student Songsheets also available on the Enhanced CD

America for Me

(with *America, the Beautiful*)

By JOHN JACOBSON
Arranged by TOM ANDERSON

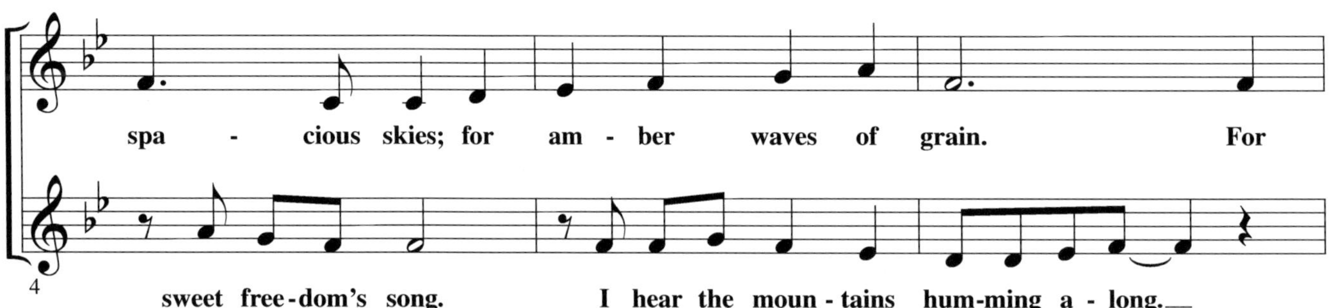

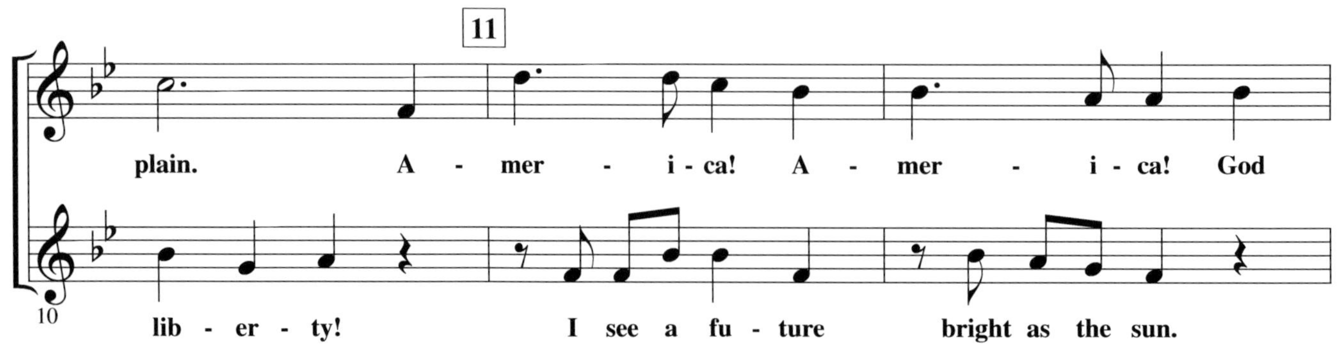

13
shed His grace on thee. And crown thy good with
I see a peo - ple liv - ing as one. Look in my heart and
16
broth - er - hood, from sea to shin - ing sea.
1
you ought to see A -
2
3
O sea to shin - ing sea.
19
mer - i - ca for me! mer - i - ca for me!

Give Love

(with *Down by the Riverside*)

By JOHN JACOBSON
Arranged by TOM ANDERSON

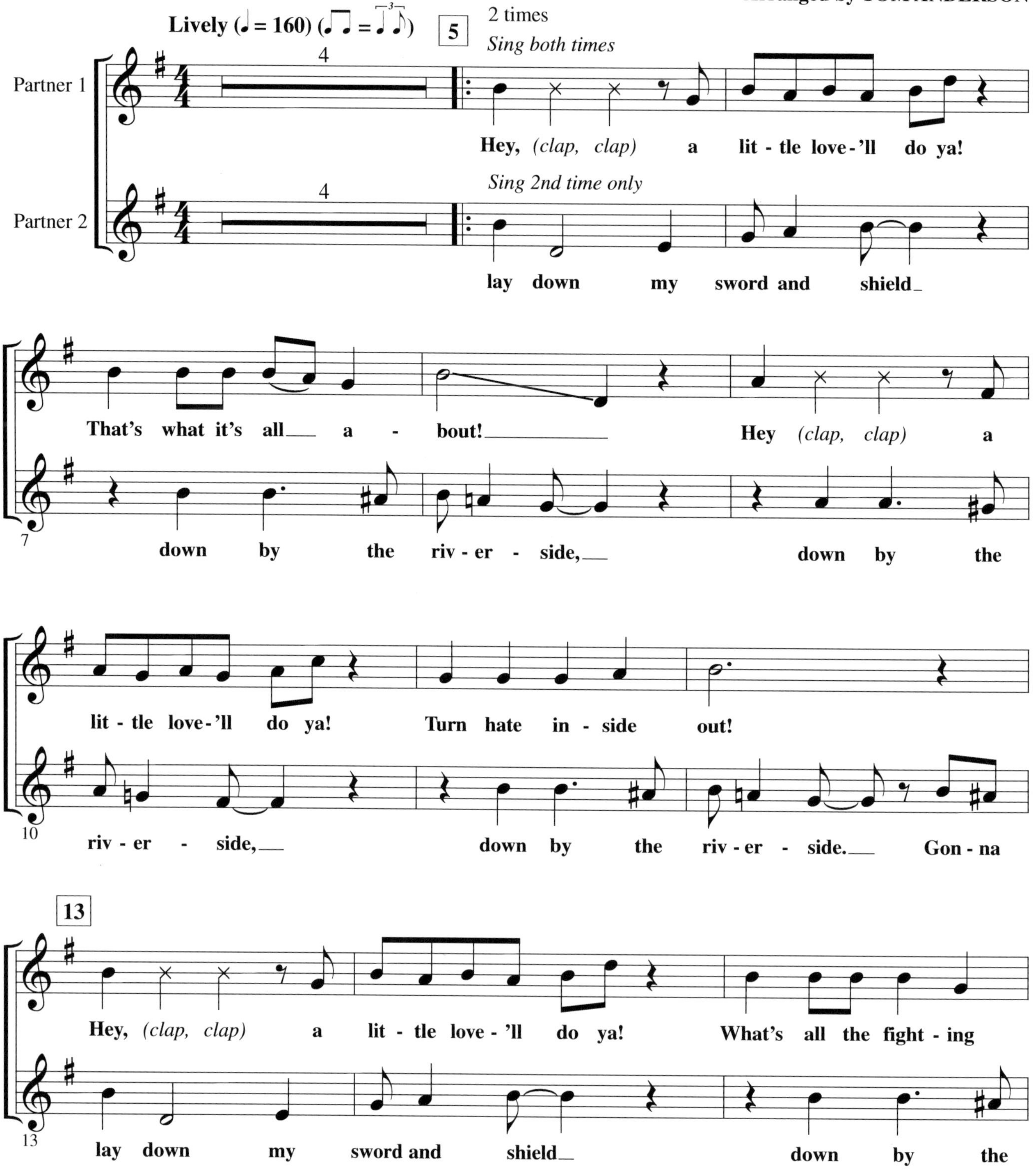

Lively (♩ = 160) (♫ = ♩♪ triplet)

5

2 times
Sing both times

Partner 1

Hey, *(clap, clap)* a lit - tle love-'ll do ya!

Sing 2nd time only

Partner 2

lay down my sword and shield

That's what it's all a - bout!

Hey *(clap, clap)* a

7

down by the riv - er - side,

down by the

lit - tle love-'ll do ya!

Turn hate in - side out!

10

riv - er - side,

down by the riv - er - side. Gon - na

13

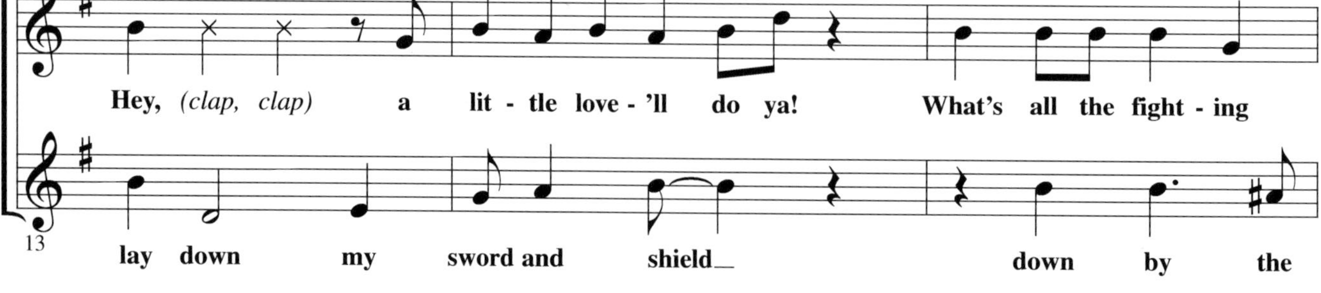

for? Oh yeah, a lit - tle love - 'll give you
16
riv - er - side and stud - y war no
21
more than a lit - tle bit more. Give love!
19
more. I ain't gon - na stud - y war no more.
Give love! Give love one more chance. Oh, won't you
22
I ain't gon - na stud - y war no more,
give love one more, one more it - ty bit - ty
25
stud - y war no more.
29
chance. Oh, won't you Give love! Give love!
28
I ain't gon - na stud - y war no more. I ain't gon - na

Give love one more chance. Oh, won't you give love
31
stud - y war no more, stud - y
one more, one more it - ty bit - ty chance!
DOWN BY THE RIVERSIDE
African-American Spiritual
34
war no Gon - na
one more it - ty bit - ty chance!
37
more.

11

Have You Ever Seen a Yankee Doodle?

(with *Yankee Doodle Boy*)

By JOHN JACOBSON
Arranged by TOM ANDERSON

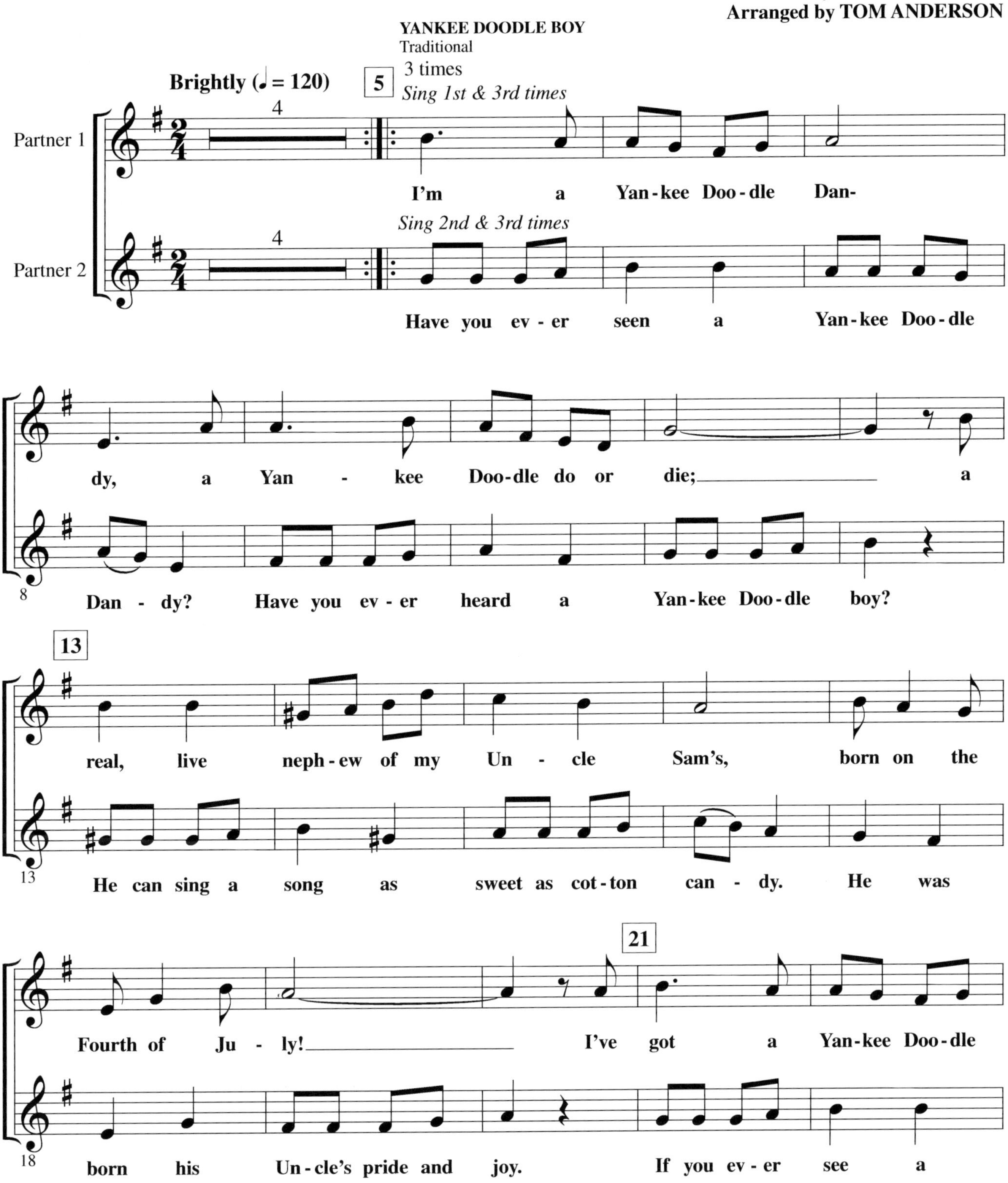

YANKEE DOODLE BOY
Traditional

Brightly (♩ = 120)

5 3 times

Partner 1 — *Sing 1st & 3rd times*
I'm a Yan-kee Doo-dle Dan-dy, a Yan - kee Doo-dle do or die; a

Partner 2 — *Sing 2nd & 3rd times*
Have you ev - er seen a Yan-kee Doo-dle Dan - dy? Have you ev - er heard a Yan-kee Doo-dle boy?

8

13

Partner 1: real, live neph-ew of my Un - cle Sam's, born on the Fourth of Ju - ly! I've got a Yan-kee Doo-dle

Partner 2: He can sing a song as sweet as cot-ton can - dy. He was born his Un-cle's pride and joy. If you ev - er see a

18

21

sweet - heart, she's my Yan - kee Doo - dle
23
Yan - kee Doo - dle Dan - dy, if you ev - er hear a
29
joy. Yan - kee Doo - dle came to Lon - don
27
Yan - kee Doo - dle boy, you will know it's
just to ride the po - nies, I am that Yan - kee Doo - dle
31
me up - on that po - ny; I am that Yan - kee Doo - dle
1
2
3
boy.
boy.
35
boy. Oh, boy! boy. Oh, boy!

I Love America

(with *Home, Sweet Home*)

By JOHN JACOBSON
Arranged by TOM ANDERSON

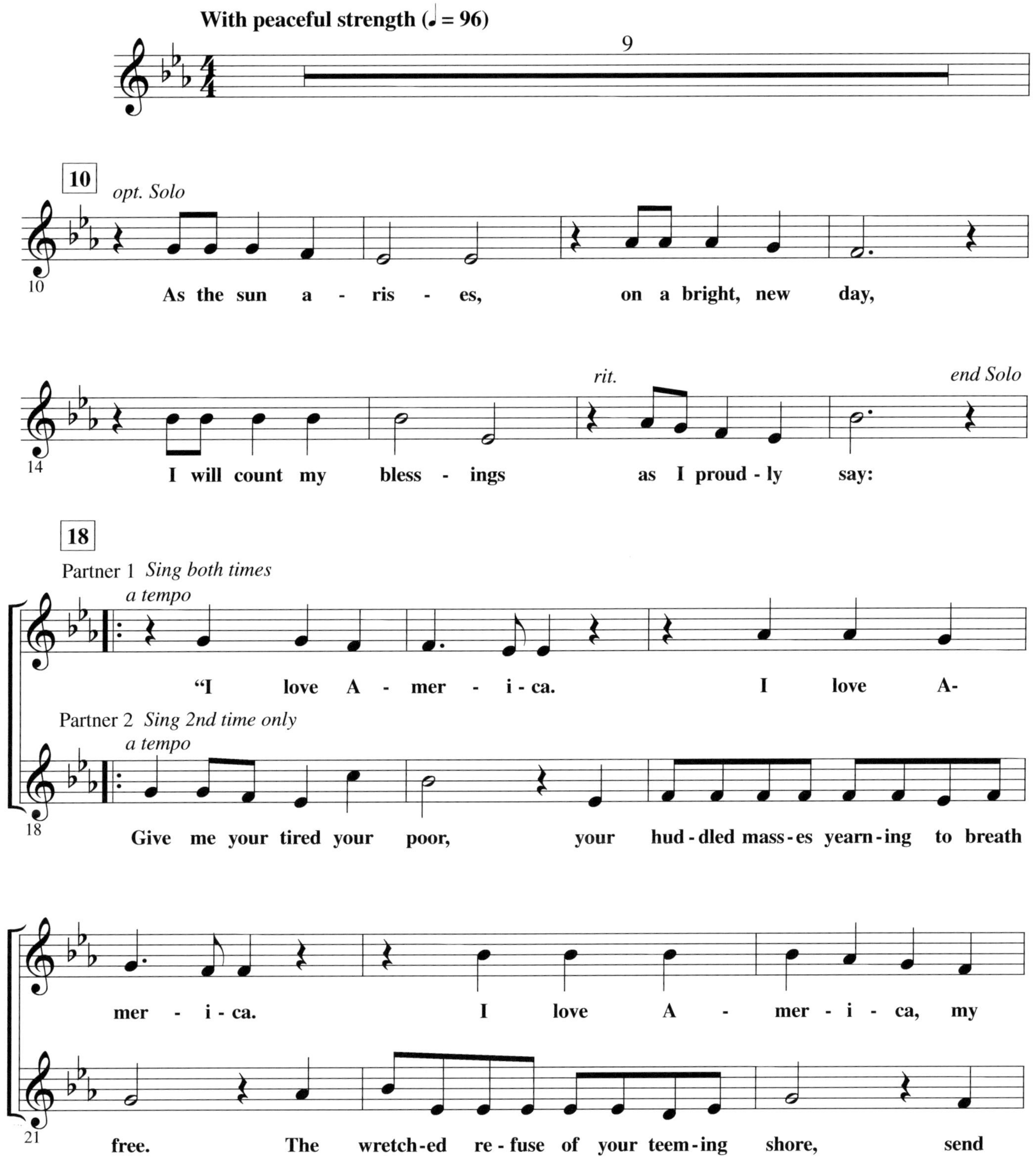

With peaceful strength (♩ = 96)

9

10 *opt. Solo*

10

As the sun a - ris - es, on a bright, new day,

rit. *end Solo*

14

I will count my bless - ings as I proud - ly say:

18

Partner 1 *Sing both times*
a tempo

"I love A - mer - i - ca. I love A-

Partner 2 *Sing 2nd time only*
a tempo

18

Give me your tired your poor, your hud - dled mass - es yearn - ing to breath

mer - i - ca. I love A - mer - i - ca, my

21

free. The wretch - ed re - fuse of your teem - ing shore, send

26
home, sweet home. I love A-
24
these, the home-less temp-est tossed to me. I lift my lamp be-side your
mer - i-ca. I love A - mer - i-ca. I love A-
27
gold - en door. I lift my lamp be-side your gold - en
1
3
mer - i-ca, our home, sweet home.”
2
home.” I love A-
31
door; wel-come home, sweet home.
mer - i-ca. I love A - mer - i-ca. I love A-
38
Home, sweet home. Home, sweet home.
mer - i-ca. I love A - mer - i-ca.
42
Home, sweet home. Home, sweet home.

I Love America

(with *Home, Sweet Home*)

MELODY INSTRUMENT

By JOHN JACOBSON
Arranged by TOM ANDERSON

With peaceful strength (♩ = 96)

10

6

16 *rit.*

18 *Play 2nd time only*

a tempo

22

26

27

32

1 *Play*

37

2

41

2

The original purchaser of this book has permission to reproduce this song for educational use in one school only. Any other use is strictly prohibited.

5/13

I Love That Grand Old Flag

(with *You're a Grand Old Flag*)

By JOHN JACOBSON
Arranged by TOM ANDERSON

YOU'RE A GRAND OLD FLAG
Words and Music by
GEORGE M. COHAN

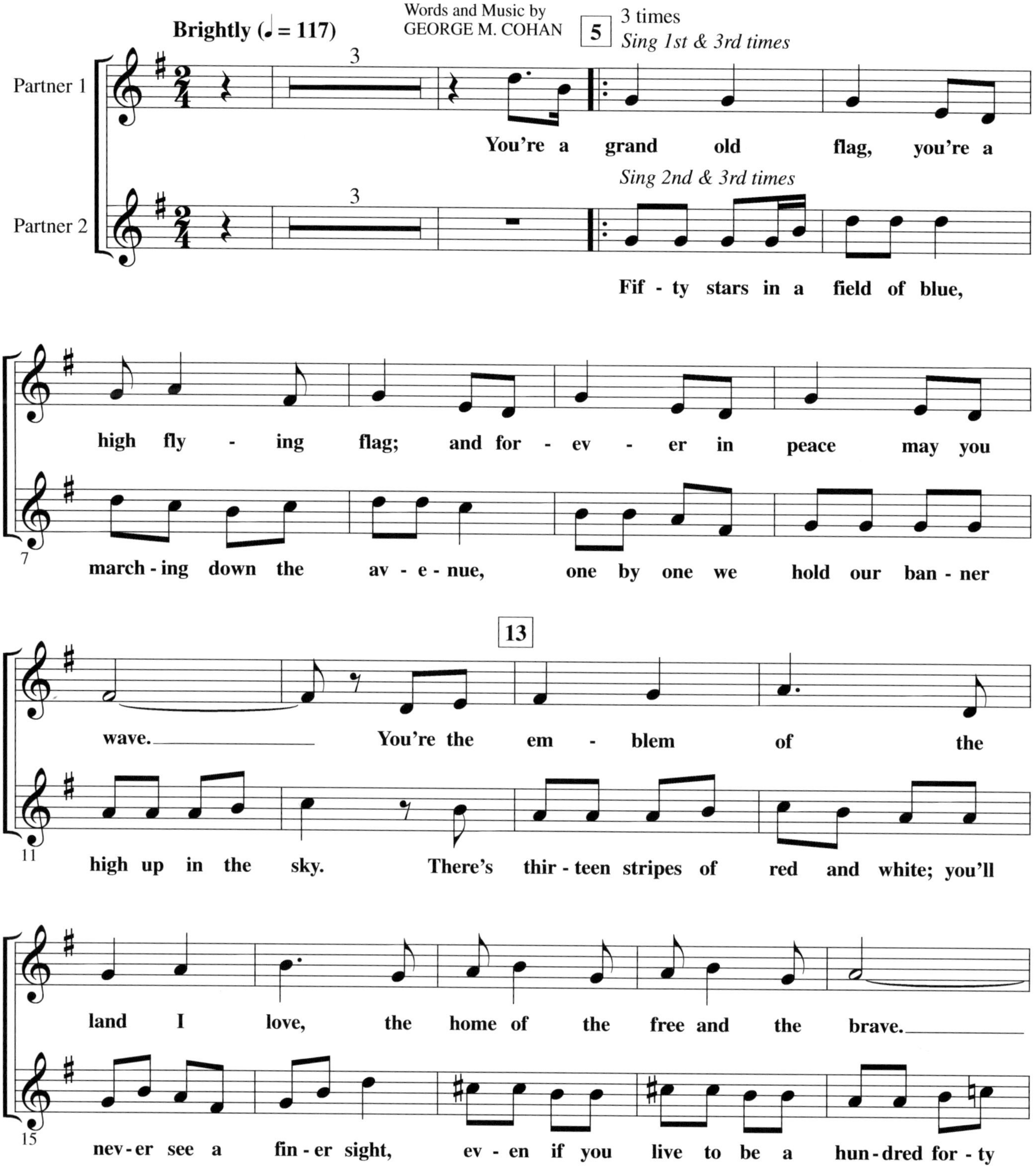

Brightly (♩ = 117)

5 — 3 times

Partner 1 — *Sing 1st & 3rd times*

Partner 2 — *Sing 2nd & 3rd times*

Partner 1: You're a grand old flag, you're a
Partner 2: Fif - ty stars in a field of blue,

Partner 1: high fly - ing flag; and for - ev - er in peace may you
7 Partner 2: march - ing down the av - e - nue, one by one we hold our ban - ner

13

Partner 1: wave. You're the em - blem of the
11 Partner 2: high up in the sky. There's thir - teen stripes of red and white; you'll

Partner 1: land I love, the home of the free and the brave.
15 Partner 2: nev - er see a fin - er sight, ev - en if you live to be a hun - dred for - ty

21
— Ev - 'ry heart beats true 'neath the red, white and
(spoken)
20
two! Whew! Proud to be an A - mer - i - can; fa - ther, moth - er,
blue, where there's nev - er a boast or brag. But should
24
daugh - ter, son! Come a - long, there's al - ways room for ev - 'ry - one.
29
auld ac - quain - tance be for - got, keep your eye on the
29
The red, the white, the blue; all right!
grand old flag.
34
I just love that grand old flag!
You're a eye on the grand old flag!
40
I just love that grand old flag!

6/14

Let Freedom Ring

(with *America*)

By JOHN JACOBSON
Arranged by TOM ANDERSON

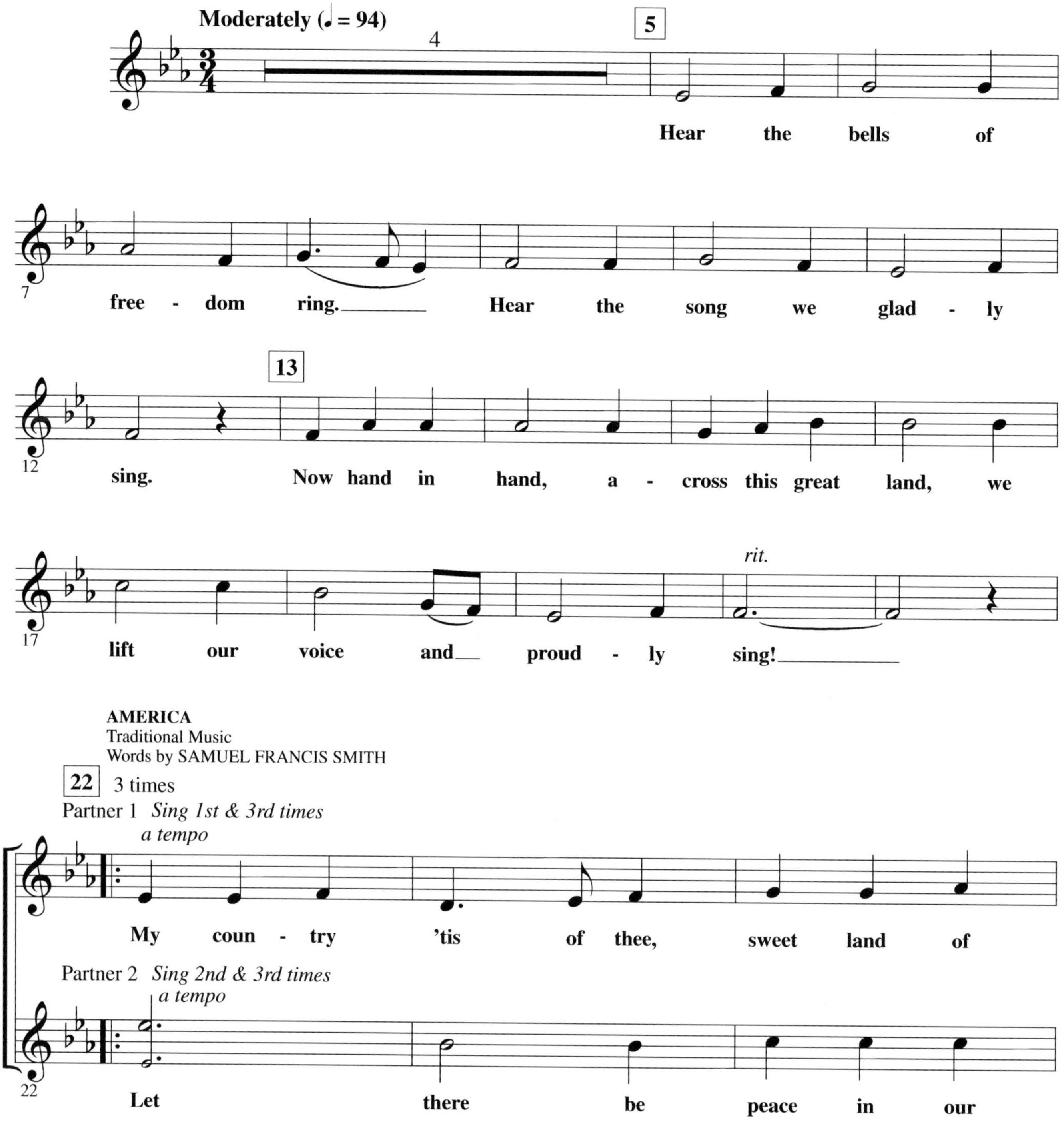

Moderately (♩ = 94)

4 5

Hear the bells of

7 free - dom ring. Hear the song we glad - ly

12 sing. 13 Now hand in hand, a - cross this great land, we

17 lift our voice and proud - ly *rit.* sing!

AMERICA
Traditional Music
Words by SAMUEL FRANCIS SMITH

22 3 times

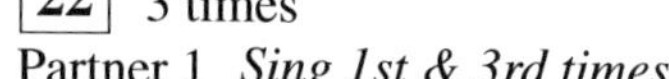

Partner 1 *Sing 1st & 3rd times*

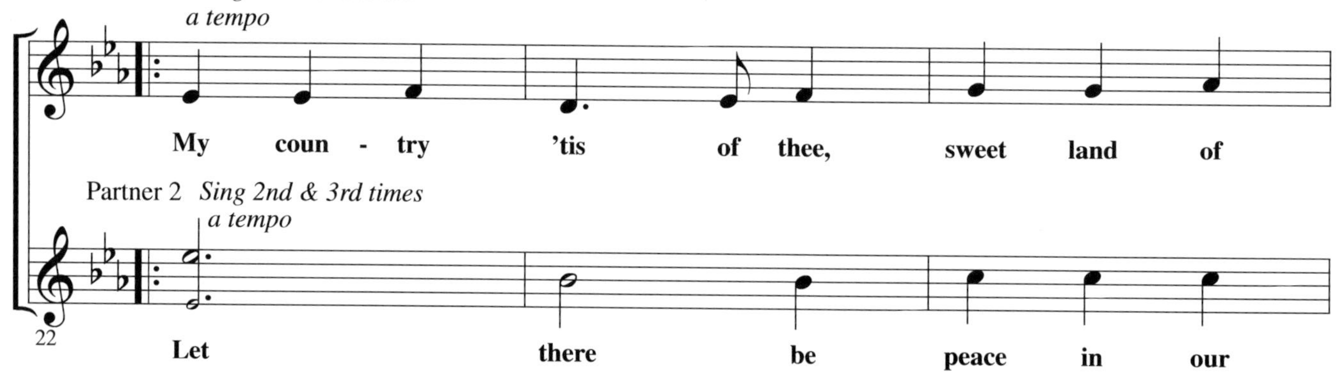

28
lib - er - ty, of thee I sing. Land where my
land. Let there be peace.
25
fa - thers died. Land of the pil - grims' pride.
Then one by one,
29
From ev - 'ry moun - tain - side, let free - dom
we shall see that we can be
32
ring. ring.
free. free.
35
45
Let free - dom ring.
We can be free.
44

Let Freedom Ring
(with *America*)

CHIMES

By JOHN JACOBSON
Arranged by TOM ANDERSON

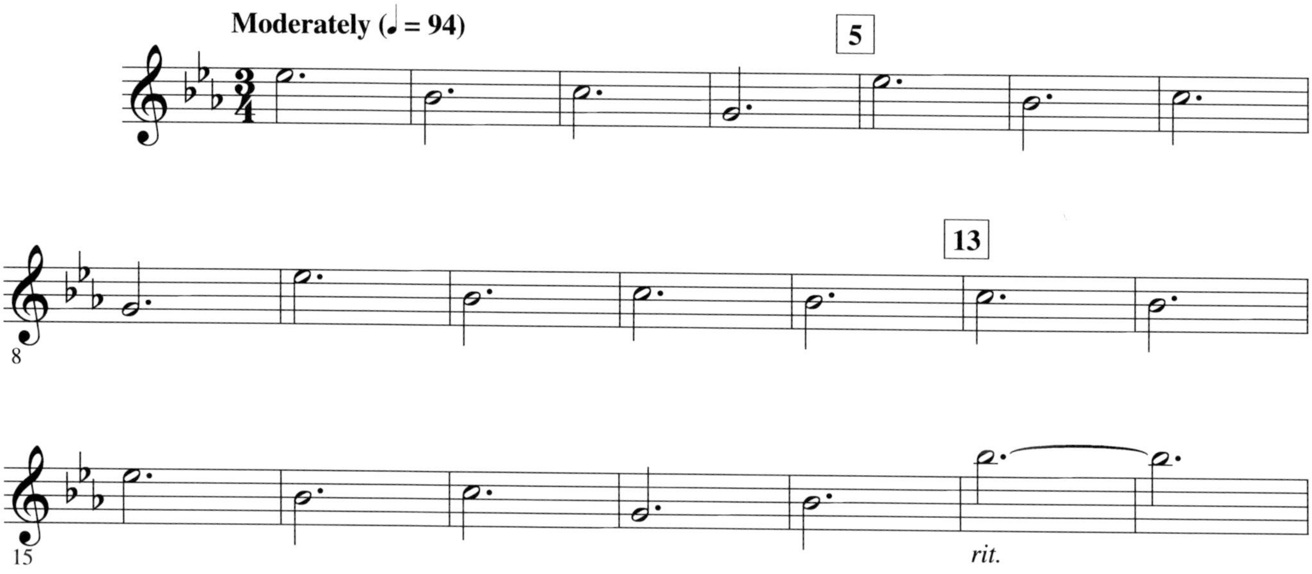

Moderately (♩ = 94)

5

13

rit.

AMERICA
Traditional Music
Words by SAMUEL FRANCIS SMITH

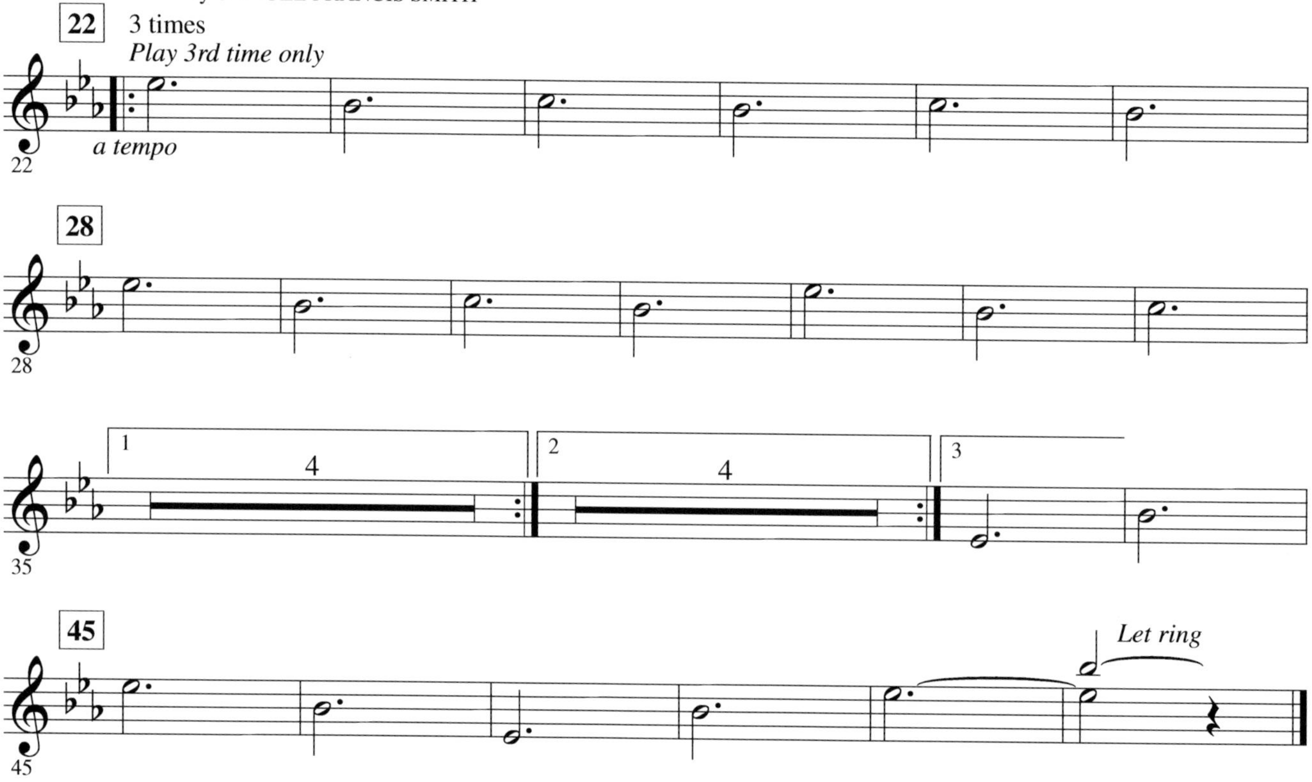

22 3 times
Play 3rd time only

a tempo

28

1 4

2 4

3

45

Let ring

7/15

There's a Light
(with *Simple Gifts*)

By JOHN JACOBSON
Arranged by TOM ANDERSON

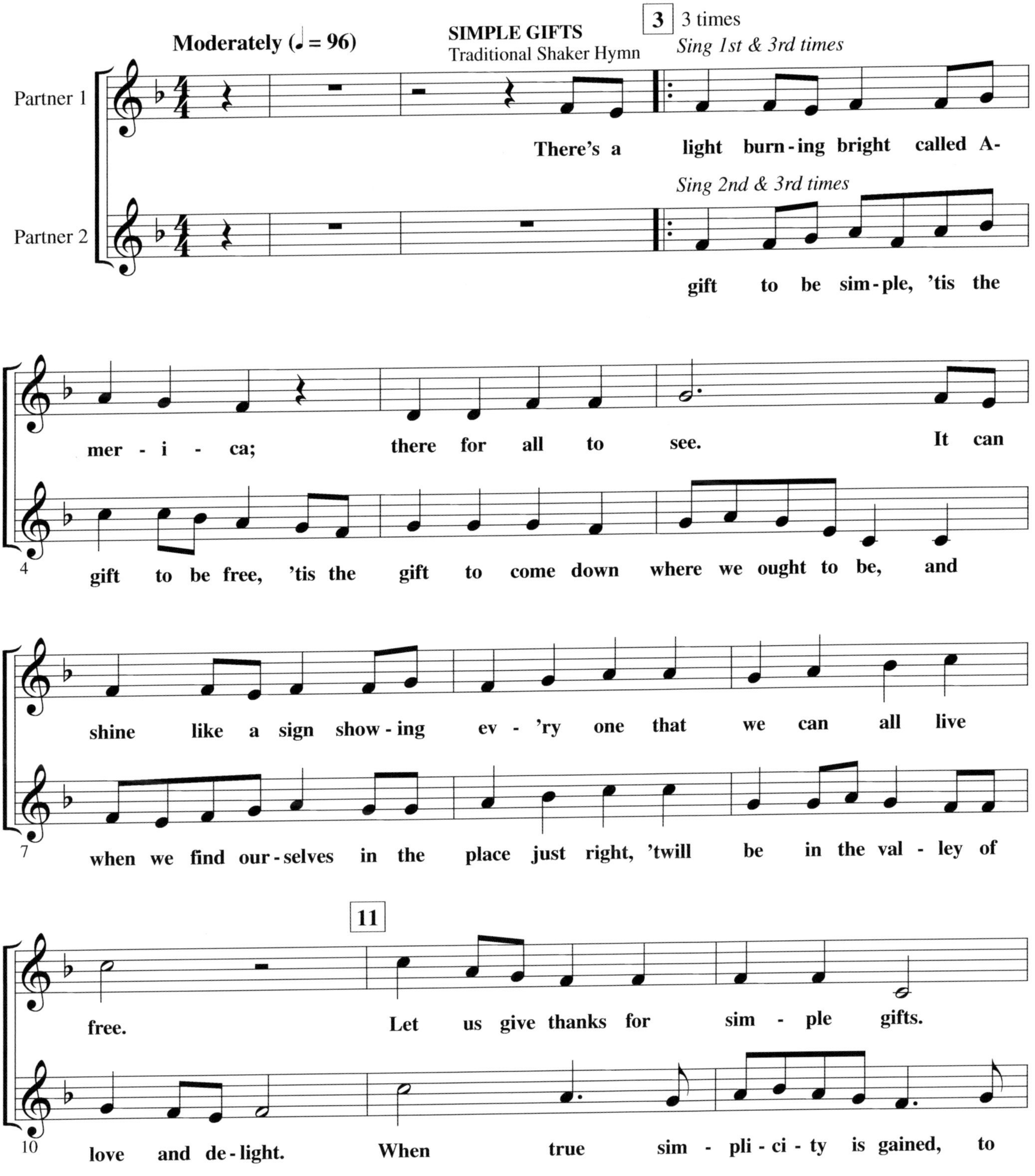

Moderately (♩ = 96)

SIMPLE GIFTS
Traditional Shaker Hymn

3 | 3 times

Partner 1 — *Sing 1st & 3rd times*

There's a light burn-ing bright called A-

Partner 2 — *Sing 2nd & 3rd times*

'Tis the gift to be sim-ple, 'tis the

mer - i - ca; there for all to see. It can

4 gift to be free, 'tis the gift to come down where we ought to be, and

shine like a sign show - ing ev - 'ry one that we can all live

7 when we find our - selves in the place just right, 'twill be in the val - ley of

11

free. Let us give thanks for sim - ple gifts.

10 love and de - light. When true sim - pli - ci - ty is gained, to

Let us give thanks for the land we love. Look in your heart and
13
bow and to bend we___ shan't be a-shamed. To turn, turn will
let your A-mer-i-can light keep shin-ing, shin-ing bright.
1
16
be our de-light, till by turn-ing, turn-ing we 'Tis the
2
3
rit. to end
There's a shin-ing bright.
rit. to end
19
come 'round right. 'Tis the come 'round right.

8/16

Three Cheers for America!

(with *Hip Hip Hooray for the U.S.A.*)

By JOHN JACOBSON
Arranged by TOM ANDERSON

4-measure drum roll-off

With pride (♩ = 120)

All shout

Hip hip hoo - ray! Hip hip hoo-

4 ray! Hoo - ray for the U. S. A.!

9 𝄋 4 times

Partner 1 — *Sing 1st & 4th times (D.S.)*

There's no place I like bet - ter than A mer - i-

Partner 2 — *Sing 2nd & 4th times (D.S.)*

"Three cheers for A - mer - i-

Partner 3 — *Sing 3rd & 4th times (D.S.)*

8 Hip hip hoo - ray for the U. S.

ca! There's no place I would rath - er stay. So

ca! Stand up proud and tall!

12 A.! Oh, hip hip hoo - ray to - day! We're proud to

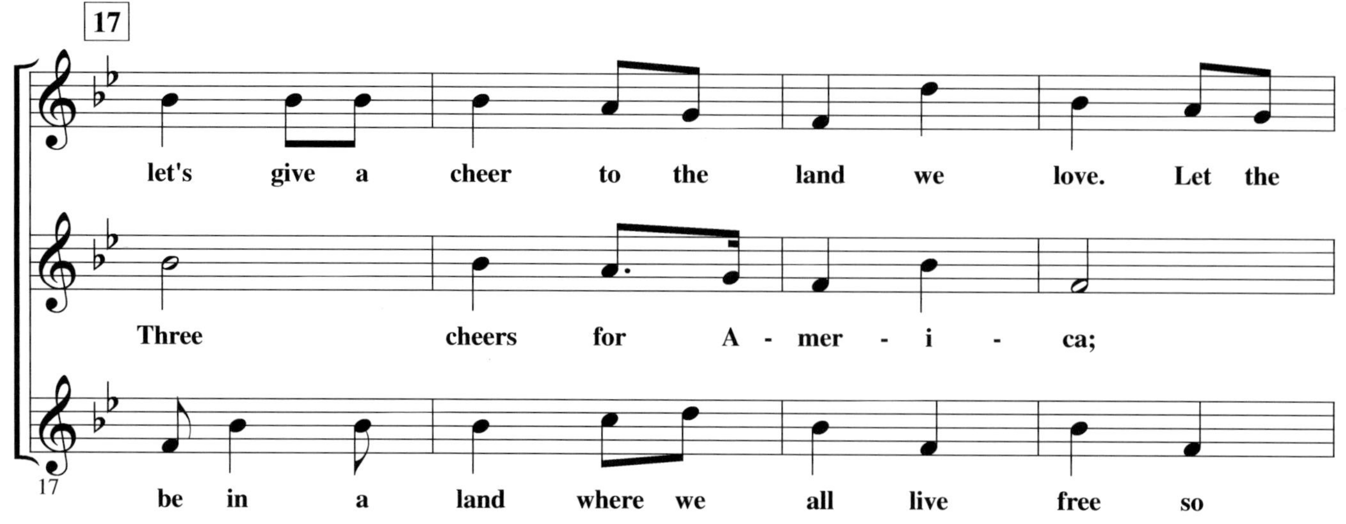
17
let's give a cheer to the land we love. Let the
Three cheers for A - mer - i - ca;
17
be in a land where we all live free so

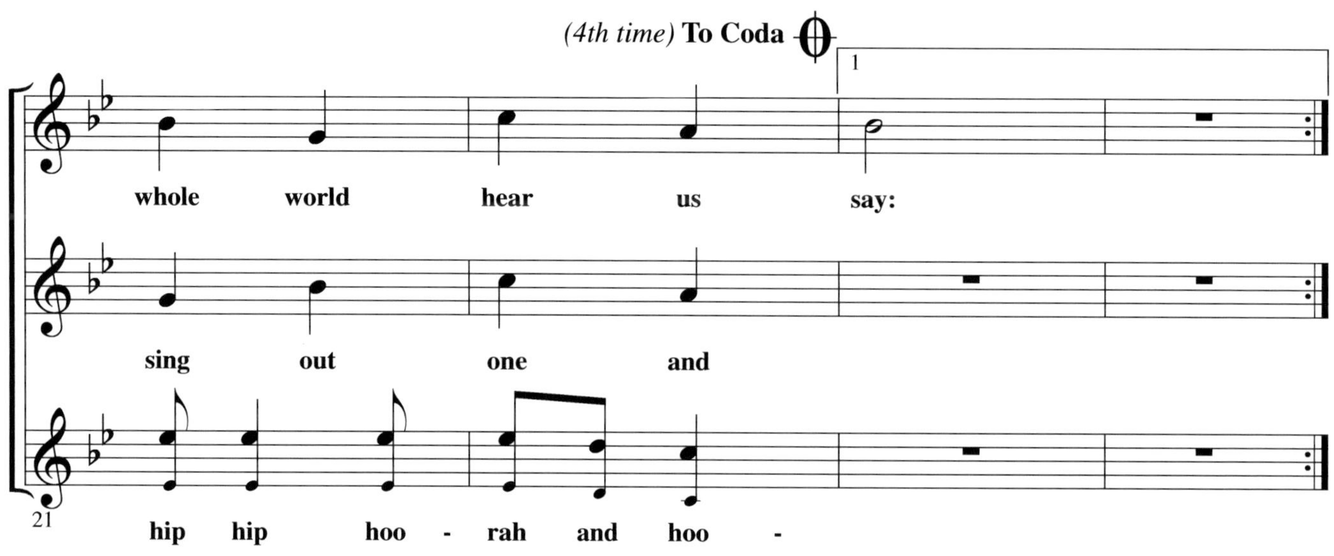
(4th time) To Coda
1
whole world hear us say:
sing out one and
21
hip hip hoo - rah and hoo -

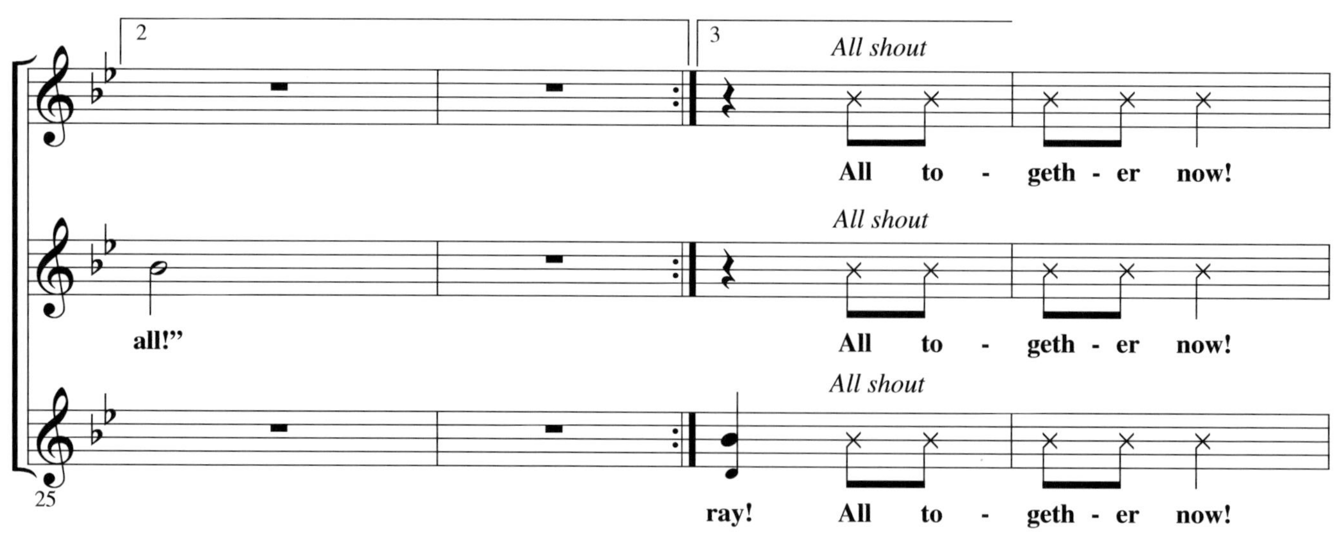
2
3
All shout
All to - geth - er now!
All shout
all!"
All to - geth - er now!
All shout
25
ray! All to - geth - er now!

29
Hip hip hoo - ray! Hip hip hoo - ray! Hoo-
Hip hip hoo - ray! Hip hip hoo - ray! Hoo-
29
Hip hip hoo - ray! Hip hip hoo - ray! Hoo-

D.S. al Coda
ray for the U. S. A.! There's
ray for the U. S. A.!
33
ray for the U. S. A.!

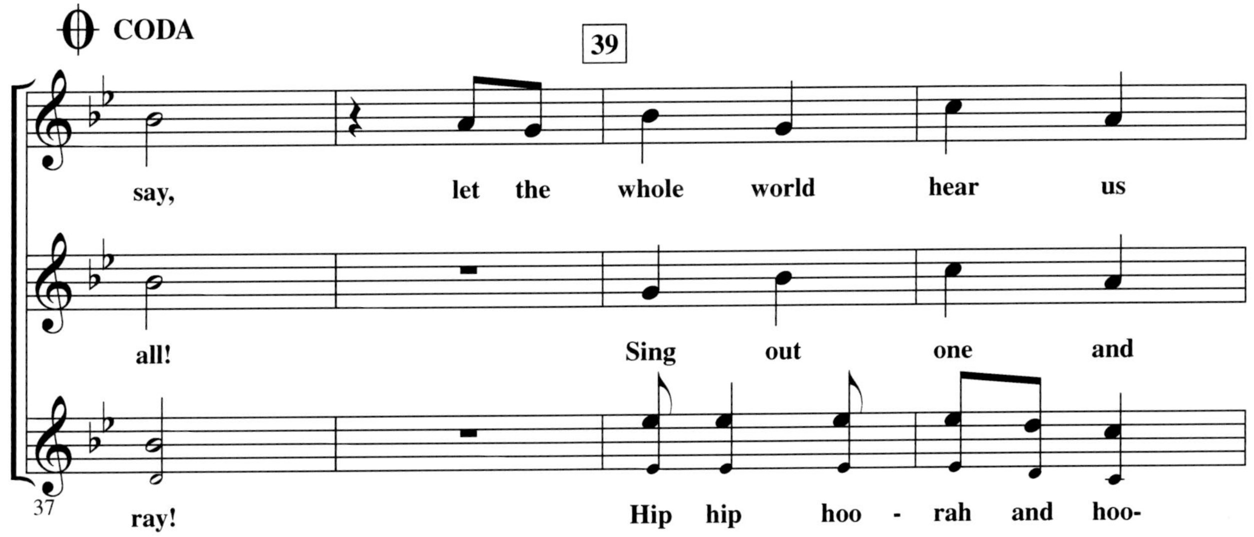
CODA
39
say, let the whole world hear us
all! Sing out one and
37
ray! Hip hip hoo - rah and hoo-

say, let the whole world hear
all! Sing out one
41
ray! Hip hip hoo - rah and

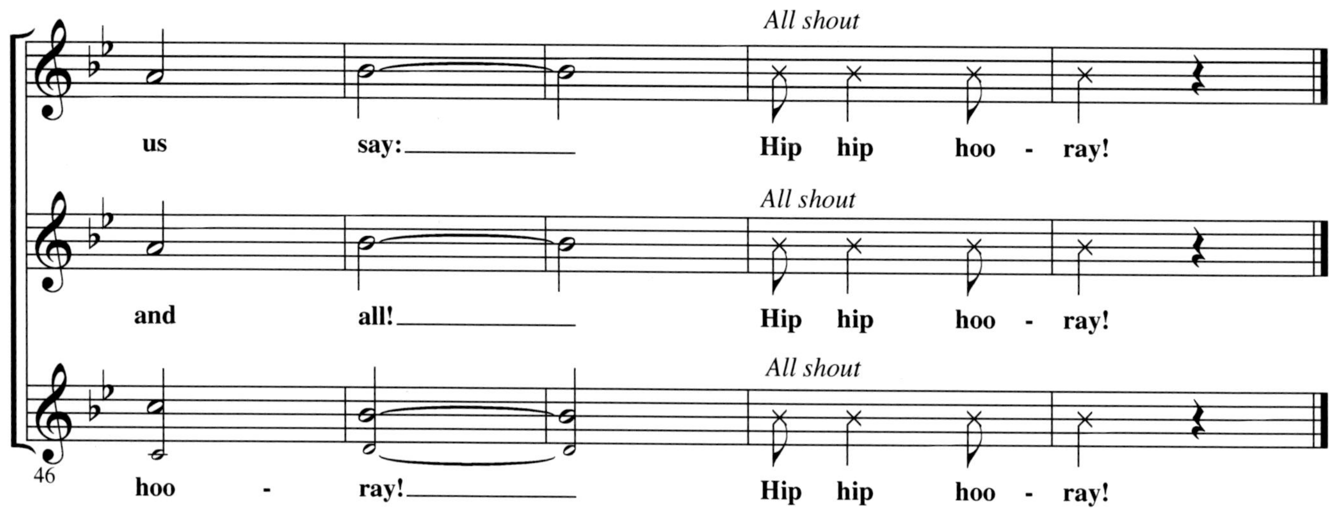
All shout
us say: Hip hip hoo - ray!
All shout
and all! Hip hip hoo - ray!
All shout
46
hoo - ray! Hip hip hoo - ray!